The Wonder of Clicker Training

The Complete Guide to a Nonviolent, Positive, Compassionate, & Effective Way of Dog Training with Clickers

James M. Meagher

Copyright© 2014 by James M. Meagher

The Wonder of Clicker Training

Publisher: Living Plus Healthy Publishing

ISBN-13: 978-1502584700

ISBN-10: 1502584700

Disclaimer

The Publisher has strived to be as accurate and complete as possible in the creation of this book. While all attempts have been made to verify information provided in this publication, the Publisher assumes no responsibility for errors, omissions, or contrary interpretation of the subject matter herein. Any perceived slights of specific persons, peoples, or organizations are unintentional.

This book is not intended for use as a source of legal, business, accounting or financial advice. All readers are advised to seek services of competent professionals in the legal, business, accounting, and finance fields.

The information in this book is not intended or implied to be a substitute for professional medical advice, diagnosis or treatment. All content contained in this book is for general information purposes only. Always consult your healthcare provider before carrying on any health program.

Table of Contents

Introduction

Shamu the killer whale weighs approximately 10,000 pounds. An Arabian horses weigh an average of 1,000 pounds. A blue-streaked parrot weighs less than a pound. And, a full-grown, adult Chihuahua has an average weight of 5 pounds.

What do these animals have in common? They can ALL be trained using a small, plastic device that weighs less than a half-pound! Surely this must be a high-tech, complex, and sophisticated device, right? Wrong!

The small device has a less than impressive name – it is commonly known as a "clicker". And, using a clicker, which fits in the palm of your hand, you can actually train animals as large as killer whales to dogs as small as Chihuahuas. This is done using some form of the popular animal training method known as "Clicker Training". Marine mammal trainers actually use a small whistle instead of a clicking device. However, the principles used for clicker training came from the training methods used to train the large marine mammals.

Clicker training is well documented to be a highly effective method of training animals. It is an amazing training protocol that has achieved almost miraculous results. Trainers of large marine mammals, such as whales and dolphins, initially used it. In fact, many of the unbelievable tricks you may have seen Shamu the killer whale perform at Sea World were taught to him using some form of clicker training.

Dog trainers have used this form of training for over 50 years. It is equally useful and effective in young puppies and older, adult dogs.

Clicker training has grown quite popular in recent years. Now widely accepted as a legitimate training protocol, it is used not only in marine mammal parks, but also in zoos, horse training facilities, and dog training schools.

The use of clicker training provides a pleasant and positive way to effectively teach animals new behaviors. This type of training is based on positive reinforcement methodology, versus the older-school methodology, which involved negative reinforcement and punishment techniques.

But, perhaps the most wonderful thing about clicker training is that it can be easily learned and used by anyone – professional trainers or non-professional pet owners! Thanks to this little tool, even the little, old lady who owns a small terrier dog can quickly and efficiently train her beloved pet.

Clicker training has opened doors to all animal owners. Through the effective use of the clicker, pets can be taught the basics, such as obedience, good manners, and even fun games. It is training that is easy to learn and easy to use, making it ideal for the whole family to get involved in the training of the family pet.

Even dog-breeders are incorporating clicker training into their businesses. Having a "clicker-ready" puppy can greatly enhance the potential to find a new owner. Knowing a new puppy has been trained with the clicker can be a great comfort to a new dog owner.

Through the use of clicker training the animal owner and the animal can enjoy a process that is fun, even exciting. Based on a positive, upbeat philosophy the animal and owner alike actually look forward to the opportunities for the animal to learn new behaviors. Instead of "dreading" another episode of tedious training, there can be enthusiasm and anticipation!

This guide to clicker training will give you an in-depth look at all aspects of this exciting method. Although this type of training can be adapted to any animal, this guide will focus primarily on dog training using the clicker.

Chapter 1: Clicker Training Basics

So, what exactly is clicker training? Simply put, it is an animal training method that involves the use of a small, mechanical device that makes a distinct click sound that lets the animal know exactly when they are doing the right thing.

What in the world is a "clicker" and where can you get one?

First, it is important to understand exactly what in the world a clicker is? To most people, the clickers used for clicker training appear to be just a small plastic toy. And, that is essentially what it is. However, when used properly to train your dog, it is a super powerful tool.

The clicker itself is most often a somewhat egg-shaped, plastic device that easily fit in the palm of your hand. It can be made of metal, but the plastic ones are usually preferred since they will not rust. The small device has a raised ball in the center that you press to elicit the distinct click sound. There is a metal strip inside the clicker that produces the click when the ball is pressed. The clicker is rather odd-looking, but ergonomically designed, so it should be comfortable to hold in your hand.

The beauty of the simple clicker is it emits a single, clear, "click" sound each time you press the ball. It is critical that the clicker produces just a single click. If it puts out a series of "clicking noises" the animal being trained can easily become confused. Most clickers on the market are designed to produce a single click.

When training animals, the clicker is used as an "event marker" to mark a desired response. The clear, unique and consistent sound of the clicker makes it an excellent event marker. The clicker training system explained below uses positive reinforcement in combination with an event marker.

Clickers can be purchased from a variety of places. Most clickers can be bought for less than five dollars. The large stores such as Walmart, Costco, etc., usually carry several types. The clickers can be easily purchased online from a number of online sites. Amazon.com has a good selection. If you do an online search for "clickers for dog training", you will find numerous websites that specialize in dog training, and many of them sell the clickers.

The type of clicker is not that important. Get one! You will be amazed that little, plastic device can help you learn what is perhaps the fastest way to train your dog to do exactly what you want him to do.

What is "clicker training"?

Clicker training is a scientifically based training method using a gentle, hands-off approach to train your dog. Many experts believe this humane and successful way of training will replace the traditional methods of dog training. It is based on a positive reinforcement philosophy. It is rapidly gaining popularity due to its simplicity, low cost, and effectiveness.

This type of training is essentially a conditioning of your dog. It "conditions" him to understand that when he hears a click, he immediately knows he has done a good thing. A thing that pleases his trainer and results in a reward for him! "Clicker conditioning" is another term often used for this type of training.

The clicker itself is not what trains the dog. Rather, the distinct click sound must be paired with something your dog likes, like food or treats. This pairing allows the dog to associate his behavior with the reward. Over time, he will learn and good behaviors will start to recur.

The clicker-training model is actually based on behavioral psychology. Its roots can be traced back to works by a Russian physiologist in the early 1900's. Ivan Pavlov has become very well known to the general public for his famous experiments on behavioral modification in dogs. Even though he was a physiologist and not a psychologist, he is perhaps best remembered for defining "classical conditioning".

Classical conditioning is a form of learning involving one stimulus called the conditioned stimulus, which causes the occurrence of a second stimulus called the unconditioned stimulus. In Pavlov's famous experiments with dogs, he presented the dogs with a ringing bell, which was his conditioned stimulus.

He followed the bell by giving the dogs food, which was the unconditioned stimulus.

The food actually caused the dogs to salivate. This was an unconditioned response. After "conditioning" the dogs by using several bell-food pairings, the bell itself also caused the dogs to salivate. This became known as a conditioned response.

In addition, clicker training is based on studies by a noted psychologist, B.F. Skinner in the 1930's. He became known as the father of "operant conditioning". This conditioning involves changing behavior through the use of reinforcement that is given after the desired response.

Skinner used pigeons in his experiments. He trained the pigeons to perform several different movements in order to receive a food reward. This was a classic example of positive reinforcement.

How does this apply to clicker training? Clicker training very effectively teaches your dog to associate a distinct sound, like the clicking sound of the clicker, with a positive reward, like a food treat. Through repeated episodes, your dog becomes conditioned, and learns that the clicker means she did wha wanted her to do at that exact instant.

Like B.F. Skinner's experiments, the clicker training system is a reward-based training method. So, your dog becomes active in the learning! And, as in Pavlov's experiments, your smart pooch learns from the conditioned stimulus (the clicker) that he will get an unconditioned stimulus (the food treat). The treat will cause the dog to learn through conditioning, such that the click causes a conditioned response – the behavior that you desire!

The clicker training method relies on marking desirable behavior and then rewarding it. The behavior is "marked" by using a clicker to tell your dog that they are doing the right thing. The clicker is used to allow the dog to quickly identify that you desire a specific behavior and what that precise behavior is. They quickly learn that if they perform that behavior, you will instantly respond with the click followed by a food treat.

A very important aspect of clicker training is to insure that the animal is promptly informed of their success, which accelerates their learning. Since it is impossible to instantly reward the behavior, the clicker serves as a "bridge" to bridge the gap between the time the dog performs the desired behavior, and the time they receive the treat.

Clearly communicating that to the dog, and then adding a positive reinforcer in the form of a treat is the essence of clicker training. It then becomes readily apparent that clicker training is, in fact, a positive, safe, humane and effective method of teaching any animal any behavior.

How is clicker training different from traditional dog training?

There are a number of differences between the training from the "old days" and clicker training.

First, and perhaps, happily, the most important, no punishment is used with clicker training methods. It is strictly positive reinforcement training. No negative reinforcement is needed during clicker training. This is an important difference between traditional dog-training methods and clicker training. With traditional methods, trainers teach dogs to perform at their command. The trainer's commands are usually in the form of eith praise or punishment.

Understandably, praise is not a punishment, but it does represent an ineffective way to train your dog. Why? Because, it takes a while for your dog to understand why it is that you are giving him treats and praise. Often, the dog is so focused on getting the reward that he "forgets" what behavior he was supposed to be learning.

Punishment on the other hand is the old school method of negative reinforcement training. The problem with the negative reinforcement models is that they teach the dog what NOT to do. These methods have been shown to be unnecessary and not very successful.

What pets learn from negative reinforcement is that if they do the undesired behavior, they will be punished. Conversely, if they do not do that undesired behavior, they will not be punished. This method of training only serves to teach the dog that you are to be feared and not trusted. The dogs may learn from this way, but they will end up only performing the behaviors you desire because they fear being punished if they do not (negative reinforcement). Not a fun way to train your dog!

On the other hand, clicker training is a gentle, hands-off, and based on positive reinforcement. The clicker is used to reward your dog for good behavior. You will simply ignore and not give any attention to their bad behavior. The quick-learning dog will realize he needs to repeat the good behaviors to reap the rewards. And, they will stop the bad behaviors because the dog learns that those behaviors will not bring any reward.

Clicker training using positive reinforcement is a much more upbeat and fun way to teach your dog. It conveys to the dog that if they do the desired behavior, they will get a reward. Not only is this much more fun for the dog and the trainer, but it also reinforces the bond between the two. Hence, trust and respect are the results. Unlike the negative reinforcement methods, clicker training becomes a fun way to teach your pet!

Second, unlike the standard training methods that would often require lengthy training sessions, clicker training involves very short sessions. Usually the training periods are only a few minutes long, avoiding long, repetitive drills that are frequently required for traditional training periods.

Third, clicker training involves the use of food treats as rewards to reinforce the positive behavior. There is no deprivation involved as in many traditional training programs.

Fourth, clicker training uses a lot of variety in its system. This variety may be in the tasks being trained, in the types of treats, in the re-inforcements used, etc. Both the animals and the trainers can appreciate the value in that!

Fifth, without question, clicker training has proven to be a much more accelerated method of leaning. Whereas traditional train-ing methods would take months or years to establish desired behaviors, using clicker training the desired results can be obtained in days or weeks. Using clicker training will def-initely speed up the learning and training pro-cess.

Lastly, the biggest difference is the clicker itself. The clicker does a number of things, but it is most powerful in its ability to interact with the animal. It allows the trainer to com-municate specific things to the dog. But, more importantly, it allows the dog to communicate back. This is extremely significant in that it al-lows the animal to think and interact using its own abilities.

Another important difference from traditional training is that the clicker is not only valuable for the animal, but also for the trainer. The clicker provides quick and effective feedback to the trainer. For clicker training to be most effective, the trainer must click exactly the behavior you want at the exact time it occurs. Using your voice, the timing is uncertain. Were you late? Early? It is difficult to determine.

However, using the clicker, the trainer can tell immediately if they were on time or not. Then, they can alter their own behavior. Hence, the feedback component of clicker training is vital to the trainer to insure their training is being done properly.

That little plastic tool, the clicker, is an amazing device. Perhaps the best thing about using the clicker in training your dog is the fact that it is non-emotional. Unlike your voice, the click produced by the clicker is the same tone and loudness every time. No human can effectively speak without emotion. If you add in the fact that you may be excited and happy when your dog performs something well, keeping your voice emotionless becomes even more difficult.

Unlike traditional training methods that use the trainer's voice, clicker training uses the clicker to produce the exact same sound every time it is activated. When "clicked" at the exact right moment, the sound of the click eliminates any confusion in the dog's mind about what behavior is being rewarded.

Because your tone of voice is often inconsistent, your voice is not an effective marker. When using the voice to train as in traditional training, the words, sounds, and tones all may sound similar to words used in regular conversations that the dog hears throughout the day. Dogs are very aware of sounds and words around them. Whether the sounds are from the television or your own voice, the sounds become like "white noise". Dogs, like humans, can tune out that noise. But, they are very keen to certain, specific sounding words, such as "treat", "toy", etc. Having a consistent, distinct sounding device like the clicker removes voice and "white noise" inconsistencies.

In addition, the distinct click sound of the clicker efficiently "marks" the event. The click conveys to your dog: "That is the correct behavior I was looking for and you will now get a reward (food treat)". Your dog will learn very quickly, and often he will try to determine what he can do to produce the click!

How to capture behaviors with a clicker

The essence of clicker training lies with the need for the trainer to "capture" specific behaviors he or she desires. As noted in Skinner's experiments, animals learn from their environment and they tend to repeat an action that has a positive consequence. Conversely, they learn very quickly not to repeat an action that has a negative consequence.

Dog trainers take advantage of this natural behavior by giving the dog positive reinforcement after the dog does something the trainer wants them to repeat. It is absolutely critical that the reinforcement must happen as the desired behavior is happening, and not afterwards. This allows the animal to connect the positive reinforcement to the behavior they are doing.

The dilemma has always been that the positive reinforcement cannot always be gotten to the animal at the exact instant they perform the behavior. The trainer strongly desires to "capture" the behavior at the time it occurs.

To capture the behavior, trainers began using conditioned reinforcers. A conditioned reinforcer is anything that the animal would not normally work to get. This differs from a primary reinforcer, which is something the dog would work to get, such as food treats. When you pair a conditioned reinforcer with a primary reinforcer, the dog will see them as equal. This is where the click of the clicker comes in as a conditioned reinforcer.

The clicker is faster than saying words like "Good dog!" The clicker allows the trainer to precisely mark or capture the behavior he wants to reinforce. When you pair the clicker with a food treat, the clicker can become a very effective tool for shaping behavior.

Actually "capturing" the behaviors you desire can be done quite simply. First, you wait for the dog to perform a certain behavior. Then, you reward it so they will repeat it. This can be done anytime and anywhere.

So, to capture your dog's behavior, you must be ready with the clicker and some food treats. Remember to work on capturing only one behavior at a time. You will confuse your dog if you try to capture multiple behaviors at a time. Keep it simple and focused.

The first step to capture a behavior is to identify the behavior you want to capture. You can choose any behavior you want your dog to perform, such as sitting, lying down, etc. Once you have decided on the behavior to capture, you simply wait and watch. The instant you observe the dog performing that specific behavior, click the clicker and give a food treat.

Always remember the mantra: "Click and treat". Not: "Treat and click". It is imperative that the click is done first, followed immediately by a treat. You always have to treat when you click, so have treats ready!

Chapter 2: Clicker Training Guidelines

Anyone who has trained any animal is very familiar with the trials and tribulations one faces when dealing with creatures that do not communicate in "human language"! We go through cycles of the "thrill of victory and the agony of defeat".

However, when basic guidelines are followed using clicker training of animals, much of the defeat is eliminated. Even if you, the trainer, "mess up" or "fail" in your handling of the clicker, it is extremely easy to recover and continue.

Perhaps it would be helpful to imbed in your brain that all types of dog training should be approached with the following "3-P Principles"

1. Patience
2. Persistence

3. Prayer

Training your dog can be fun, rewarding and productive if you keep these in mind. Remember, it is a process, not a one-step deal.

The treats!

All dog owners are well aware of the strong emotions that can be elicited from their dogs by the mere mention of the word "treat" (or any variation thereof!). Food treats are very effective rewards for all dogs. Used properly, they become very powerful motivators during training.

The basic foundation of clicker training lies in the concept of "click and "**treat**". Therefore, it is imperative that the trainer is familiar with the various types of treats recommended for the clicker training method. The "correct" treat to use is really anything your dog likes and, more importantly, will actively work to get.

There are numerous types of treats that can be used. Perhaps you have seen "show dogs" being led around the arena and then rewarded with some type of very small treat from their handlers. Clicker training treats should be similar to these types of treats.

In general, experts agree on a few recommendations for selecting food treats for the "click and treat" phase of clicker training.

Bite-sized treats:

Now, this recommendation certainly is dependent on the size of dog you have. A bite-sized treat for a five-pound Papillion puppy would be drastically different than a bite-sized treat for a two hundred-pound Great Dane! So use your head and use discretion when determining the appropriate "bite size" for your pooch.

Soft texture:

Most everyone agrees that the food treats need to have a soft texture. Avoid crunchy or chewy treats. These types of treats tend to make the dog temporarily shift its focus from the training that is occurring to chewing the treat. When their focus is disturbed, even for a few seconds, it can affect the effectiveness of the training session.

Easy to swallow whole:

Again, to prevent a loss of focus, the treats need to be easy to swallow in one gulp. So, tailor your bite-size to your dog's size so they can easily swallow the small treats.

Favorite treats:

This is a great suggestion since you already know your dog likes the treat. It may be her favorite kibble from her daily meal food. Although, this may not be the best, since these may be crunchy and require chewing. Any favorite treat that is soft and bite-sized would be a good choice.

Examples of types of treats:

Really, any small, moist treats are suitable. Tiny bits of chicken are often very good choices for "click and treat". Insure no bones are present and cut the chicken into very small bits. The soft texture and good flavor make this a good treat to use.

Very small pieces of hot dogs work well, too. Many dogs like cheeses. Small morsels of their favorite cheese will work. Any treats that are tasty are great.

Another consideration when deciding what kind of treats to use is to try to select something that your dog does not get very often. If you can make the training treats something unique, you will automatically give the dog an added incentive to perform for you during their training sessions. You can really motivate your pup with very tasty and special treats. You can make it even better if you add variety. One session with hot dog pieces and the next with cheese. Be creative.

Store-bought, ready-made treats:

There are numerous places to purchase ready-made treats to be used for training dogs. Online resources abound. The large pet stores like PetSmart and Petco carry lots of varieties. Just be sure to check the size and texture of the treats before you buy. Be sure they are appropriate for your dog.

You do not have to buy the ready-made treats. You may be able to save some money by making your own at home. Boil some chicken. Cut up some cheese. Just follow these guidelines for the appropriate treats, and you will have great treats to use for your training sessions.

Special note:

Keep in mind that you are not encouraging you dog to become a fat, overweight, obese dog. Use some common sense and keep the treat sizes small and healthy. Yes, this can be done with a little forethought and preparation in advance. The sole purpose of the treat is to immediately reinforce the click.

Additionally, remember your dog is active and working while training. This physical activity helps offset the calorie intake they get from the treats. That good exercise, combined with the fact that this type of training is very stimulating for the dog, means you really need not worry about the dog over-eating.

Another tip when thinking about the "extra" calories is to consider doing your training sessions in place of a mealtime. That way you are not feeding your dog any more food than they normally eat.

Proper Handling of the clicker during training – "Clicker Mechanics"

To the untrained clicker trainer, this may sound somewhat elementary and basic. Why would anyone need to learn the "proper handling" of this small, plastic gadget? Don't you just press the raised ball and make it click?

The simple answer to that is yes. However, when training with the clicker, handling the clicker can be a little tricky. The proper handling is easy to master, but it does take some practice on the part of the trainer. Putting some time into this prior to your first training session will pay huge dividends when you start the actual training with your pup!

The skills necessary to properly handle the clicker are actual physical or mechanical skills. Hence, these skills are frequently referred to as clicker mechanics. To get the absolute most out of clicker training your dog, you must be able to put together several simple mechanical skills. This may sound daunting, but these skills are simple and easy to learn. The tricky, but essential, part is putting them all together during the actual training sessions.

We have all learned physical skills that required multiple, simple mechanical movements, that when put together, produced a wonderful result after practice. Sports are a classic example. In baseball, for instance, one must learn to observe the pitcher, watch the ball as it approaches, time the movement of the hands to swing the bat, hit the ball, drop the bat and run! Ballet dancing is another example. The intricate movements, musical timing, and physicality all must be learned with practice.

When all these movements are practiced and learned, the eventually flow with ease. That is also true for the simple mechanics you must learn for clicker training. The skills you must learn all overlap when put into use and flow nicely together to allow you to properly handle the clicker.

There are a number of physical skills you must master before you even start training with your dog. Do not get discouraged. You will feel awkward at times. Like learning any new skill, at first, your timing will not be right. You will feel more comfortable and more confident with time. Remember that once you have learned these skills, they will come naturally.

Why is it necessary and important to master clicker mechanics? The actual click sound from the clicker is what "marks" the behavior. That is the essence of clicker training. That click conveys critical information to your dog: "Yes, that is the correct behavior." And, since a positive reinforcer like a food treat is delivered after the click, the dog very rapidly learns that the behavior she was performing when she heard the click sound will be followed by a treat.

More importantly, if you are handling your clicker to time your click well, your pup will know exactly which behavior to repeat in order for him to get more clicks and treats. And, that is your goal when training any animal – to teach them to consistently repeat the behavior you want.

Therefore, mastering clicker mechanics gives you, the trainer, the ability to become more skilled at conveying a clear and concise message. And, equally important, you learn to avoid unnecessary movements or white noises that serve only to lessen the impact of that message.

You can train yourself with some simple and fun exercises. It is important to practice these exercises *without your dog present*. You do not want to confuse your dog with your own practice using the clicker. Practice these with a friend, or even by yourself.

Here are some exercises to learn better clicker mechanics:

1. Get used to the clicker itself.

There are several different types of clickers available. These are relatively inexpensive little gadgets. So, an important thing to remember is that if one does not seem to be working or seems to frighten or startle your dog, then try another. Each different brand produces a different sounding click. One may work better than another for you and more importantly, for your dog.

Clicking the clicker:

As silly as this may sound, practice actually making the clicker click! Hold the device in your right and left hand. Which feels more comfortable? Press the clicker button using your thumb, palm of your hand, and index finger. Which allows you to produce a consistent sound? Even changing the position of the clicker in your hand can make it more comfortable. Click several times using different hands.

It may be helpful to purchase an inexpensive, elastic lanyard or wrist coil to attach to the clicker. This allows you to keep track of the clicker since it is attached to your wrist.

Some people prefer this, whereas others feel it is a little too cumbersome. Use whichever is comfortable for you.

How to click the clicker:

Press and release the clicker button quickly. The sound needs to be a short, distinct click. The sound produced from the clicker really does vary depending on how fast you press and release the button. Shoot for a quick press that produces a consistent sound every time you do it.

Exercises in clicking:

The importance of learning to properly click the clicker comfortably so it produces a consistent-sounding click will become evident as you progress in your clicker training. Some experts even recommend recording yourself clicking the clicker. Whether or not your record yourself, practice clicking the clicker 20-25 times. Do this using your thumb, then your index finger, and then your palm. Repeat this exercise until you produce a consistent sound and length from the clicker.

Once you feel comfortable pressing the clicker, begin timing yourself. Your goal should be to produce twenty consecutive, consistent clicks in twenty seconds. Keep practicing until you can do this. It will not take long for you to get to that point.

2. Practice being still.

This, too, may sound ridiculous. But, being still is not something we do easily. We are constantly pulling at our ears, rubbing our face, playing with our hair, etc., often subconsciously. In clicker training, it is vitally important for the trainer to learn to keep his body still during training sessions.

Often you will get discouraged because you feel your dog just is not getting it when you are clicker training her. It may very well be that they are not able to focus or get it because you may be exhibiting too much extraneous movement with your hands, arms, etc. These movements can be very distracting to the dog. So, you must practice remaining motionless.

The only two movements you need to make during clicker training are the pressing of the clicker and the delivery of the treat.

Remember, giving the treat has to be a separate action from the actual click.

Your clicker hand:

It is not necessary to point the clicker at the dog when you click. As a matter of fact, you must not do that. That can confuse him. He will likely focus on your hand that is pointing the crazy plastic clicking device at him. There is no need to act as if the clicker is a remote control device that needs to be pointed at the dog to be effective.

It is recommended that you keep the clicker out of view of the pet as you hold it motionless in the palm of your hand. The less movement, the less distraction. There will be slight movement as you press the clicker. But, keep even that small movement as minimal as possible.

Your treat hand:

Keeping this hand motionless is even more important than your clicker hand. Why? Because it is critical that the dog focuses on the sound of the click and not on the treat he is going to receive.

Keep the click separate from your reaching for the treat bag. Click, then move your treat hand to get the treat and deliver it to the dog. If you are moving to get a treat from the treat pouch at the same time you are clicking, any savvy dog will focus only on that treat hand going for the good stuff, and not on the click.

Your arms:

Keep both arms at your sides and motionless. This is a very difficult habit to develop since we love to clap or raise our hands victoriously when our wonderful pooch does the behavior we want. But, remember, we want to avoid extraneous distractions. Keep your arms still and at your sides.

Exercises in motionless:

Repeat the clicking exercises described above, but this time practice doing them in different positions. Standing, hold your arms motionless at your side and keep your hands still. No movement. Run through each exercise like this. Then repeat sitting with your hands on your lap.

These exercises are easy and quick. But, they are essential. Doing these exercises will make you aware of what you are doing with your body so you can control your potentially distracting movements during training sessions. Fewer distractions mean better focus for both you and your dog.

3. Practice keeping your eyes on your dog!

To learn how to properly handle the clicker during training, it is imperative that you constantly observe your dog's behavior. Clicking to mark the correct behavior is the core of clicker training. If you are distracted and looking elsewhere, you can miss the behavior, and hence, miss the click and treat opportunity. This can interrupt the flow of the session and confuse your pet.

4. Practice clicking the exact correct behavior.

As discussed earlier, marking the correct behavior is what the clicker does. Practicing your clicker expertise in clicking a specific behavior is super important for successful clicker training.

Honing this skill so you are clicking at the precise moment the correct behavior is performed will insure that your dog knows exactly what behavior earned her the treat. Then, she will know that is the behavior to repeat to get that wonderful click and treat. Clicking too soon or too late will only introduce confusion in her dog brain.

Exercises in observing and clicking at the correct time:

There are innumerable, fun exercises you can do to help you learn proper timing of your clicks. Almost all dog trainers recommend the bouncing ball exercise.

Get a friend or family member to assist you. Use a rubber ball or tennis ball. Have your friend bounce the ball at various heights. First, practice clicking as the ball reaches the ground. Practice this several times. Then, practice clicking as the ball reaches the top of its trajectory – before it starts to fall back to the ground. Repeat several repetitions.

You can even practice by having your friend perform various behaviors and you click whenever they do that desired behavior. For example, every time they turn their head to the right, you click. Have them vary their head movements so you get used to only clicking the desired behavior – the right turning head!

Another very effective way to practice this is to go to YouTube and watch any basic dog training video. Only watch them with no sound. Whatever the trainer is teaching the dog to do, you practice clicking whenever the dog does that behavior – sitting, lying down, rolling over, etc.

Remember to also practice keeping your body and arms and hands still while you are doing these exercises.

These exercises are excellent ways to improve your timing and your observational skills. Both of these are essential to properly clicker train your dog. When you feel comfortable with your newfound observation and timing skills, congratulate yourself and move on! Soon your pooch will be joining you.

5. Practicing "click and treat".

Remember to keep that sequence in mind at all times. First, the click, and then the treat. Not vice versa. One click, one treat is also important. If you make a mistake and click at the wrong time, you must still treat. It is important to implant in your dog's mind that positive reinforcement always follows the click. Consider your click as your promise to your pup that you will give a treat. And, you don't want to break your promises!

The click and treat action needs to not overlap. Be conscious of first clicking. Then, make the motion to get the treat to the dog.

Exercises in clicking and treating:

Take this in simple steps. It is very helpful if you follow this recommended sequence, even if it sounds too simplistic. Set a bowl on a table. Get twenty dried beans (to simulate your dog's food treats). Put the treats in your treat pouch at your side.

Initially, practice without the clicker. Get used to the motions of taking a treat out of the pouch and delivering it to the bowl on the table. Do this for each of the twenty beans. Repeat this several times. Remember to practice keeping your other hand/arm motionless and returning your treat hand to your side between each delivery.

Next, replace the beans in the pouch and get your clicker and a timer. Your goal will be to click and treat all twenty treats from your pouch to the bowl in thirty seconds. Have fun with this. It sounds easy, but will take some practice, especially if you concentrate on remaining motionless.

Click the clicker, then get a treat from the pouch and place it in the bowl. Return to stillness. Click and deliver another treat. Return to stillness. Do this for all twenty treats. Check your time. Don't rush to beat the clock. Rather, practice until your flow comes easily, and you can deliver all of them in thirty seconds. This may take several tries, but do it until you feel very comfortable.

What's the big deal about twenty treats in thirty seconds? This tells you that you are able to deliver a treat to your dog's mouth very quickly after you have clicked the correct behavior. That time of delivery is important to successful results with clicker training.

You can take this even one step further by using a YouTube video with no sound as described above. Practice clicking the dog's behavior and then delivering your treat to the bowl. Some dog training websites even have videos just for this purpose. These give you a much better feel for "working" with a dog than just clicking and putting beans in a bowl.

Practice with these "silent" dogs and have some fun!

Timing is of the essence!

One last guideline that is important to emphasize is timing. It is vital to learn to click *during* the desired behavior. If you wait to click until the behavior is completely finished, you will likely be too late with the click. Practice clicking during the behavior.

Although both are important, the timing of the click is what is more crucial than the timing of the treat. The click *ends* the behavior, so give the treat after the behavior! It is not uncommon for your dog to stop the behavior when it hears the click, that's okay. Give the treat. Remember the click ends the behavior.

Keep in mind that the click acts a bridge. Because the clicker puts out a clear and distinct sound every time, that sound helps bridge the time between when you mark the desired behavior to when you deliver the reward. It is only a few seconds, but if there is not a bridge, the dog can lose focus and potentially misunderstand why he is being rewarded.

The clicker immediately tells the dog "Job well done"! So, he gets that same message every time you mark the precise moment he performs that behavior with a click. The click is much faster than any verbal praise. The click helps dog understand that they did a correct behavior, the click signifies the end of that behavior, and a treat is on its way. So the click gives you some leeway between the behavior and the reward.

Another aspect of timing concerns the length of the training sessions. Keep the sessions short. Five to ten minutes are usually adequate when repeated throughout the day. This prevents boredom from setting in for the dog and trainer alike. The shorter sessions also help to keep the dog focused, motivated and excited. More fun for all!

Practicing these guidelines as part of your preparation for clicker training can be fun! It may seem tedious, but be silly and laugh at yourself when you make awkward mistakes. Correct the mistakes and move on. This is not rocket science. Your goal is to train yourself - so you can train your dog – so you can both have some fun together!

Now you can add the best part – your wonderful dog!

Chapter 3: Getting Started

Once you feel you have mastered the exercises and you feel confident in handling the clicker, you can move on to put that training to work on your dog. Your confidence will be very reassuring to your dog and make the entire clicker training experience exciting.

Preparing for each training session

A very helpful tip is to make time to prepare yourself for each training session. Simple preparations will most certainly make the flow into training much smoother.

Gather your necessary tools. Get the clicker (and wrist lanyard, if you are using one). Prepare your small, bite-sized treats or collect some of your purchased treats. Place all the treats into your pouch.

Decide on what behavior you plan to click at that session. Do a little mental review of your clicker mechanics and how you will use them for this particular behavior training session.

Select an appropriate location for the session. If at all possible, the location should be quiet and free of distractions. If outdoors, pick a spot that does not have squirrels running around or the neighbor's cat lurking in the bushes. Also, try to find a spot free of other humans. Their talking can be distracting.

If you are indoors, find a place with enough space. Clear any dog toys from the dog's sight. If you have other pets, take care of relocating them before you start your session. Turn off the television and radio.

Pick the right time to conduct your training session. Do not try your clicker training on a tired pooch. Pick a time when she is well rested and ready to learn. Perhaps even more important is to select a time around her normal mealtime. Do not try to do the training right after the dog has eaten a meal. The small, bite-sized treats you will use during training offer a lot less motivation to a dog with a full tummy. Stack the odds in your favor by planning your sessions when you have an alert, hungry dog.

Your preparations are critical. You and your dog can have a great time together during the sessions when you, the trainer, are well prepared.

Preliminary Step – "Loading" or "Charging" the clicker

A critical step, and one that must be done as a first step when working with your dog, is to introduce the clicker to them. Your dog has no idea what the clicker is or what a click means. You want to immediately teach your pooch to associate the sound of the clicker with something good happening to her. You are going to develop a very strong "stimulus-response" system through this loading step.

The concept of introducing the dog to the clicker is known as "loading the clicker" or "charging the clicker". These may seem like odd terms. How in the world do you "load" or "charge" a small, plastic toy clicker?

The concept simply means you must introduce the clicker, the sound of the click, and the positive reinforcer repeatedly to the dog.

This loading procedure insures that your dog associates the clicking sound with a delicious treat! The following steps will insure that your dog's brain will be loaded or charged with the concept of click and treat. This is a conditioning process – you repeat it until she is conditioned to the sound of the clicker.

As an aside, if you have a fearful dog or one that is easily startled, you may try to hold the clicker in your pocket to mute reduce the loudness of the click.

Training steps to load the clicker:

This is a very simple, but vital part of clicker training. All remaining steps depend on this foundational process.

You do not introduce any specific behaviors when loading the clicker. Your sole purpose is to introduce the clicker sound and the tasty treats to develop that association. So, gather your treats in your treat pouch. Using the same pouch for every training session allows for an added level of comfort for your dog.

All you need to load the clicker is the pouch with the food treats, the clicker, and, of course, your pup! With your pet nearby, click the clicker and immediately give him a treat from your pouch. Be sure you do it as you practiced during your clicker mechanics – practice being still and establishing the proper sequence. Also, remember to do these sessions when the dog is hungry.

Be sure your dog is not doing something that you do not want to reinforce. Then click, and treat. Click, then treat. Repeat this several times. Be advised, Fido is not earning these treats. He will consider this his lucky day. All you do is click and treat. His dog brain will be quickly loaded or charged with associating that wonderful new clicking sound with a delicious food treat!

Do this with ten treats at a session. Repeat this session three to four sessions a day. If you are doing it while the dog is on a leash, hold the clicker in the leash hand so you can readily retrieve a treat from the pouch and deliver it to the dog with your free hand.

After a few of these sessions, check to see if your dog is "loaded". Wait for a time during the day when he is not paying attention to you or he is distracted. Be sure you have a treat ready, and click the clicker. If he looks at you or comes toward you, give him a treat. He is "loaded".

Even if he does not respond to the clicker, go to him and give him a treat to implant in his mind that every time there is a click there is a treat. This simply means that he is not "loaded" yet, and you will need to do a few more sessions of click and treat.

When you feel he is "loaded", start decreasing the number of sessions. Once fully "loaded", you can proceed with all the other exciting clicker training sessions.

The "loading" process is very enjoyable and rewarding for the trainer. It is so exciting and fun to watch what happens as you see the dog begin to "get it". You will get rapid feedback that clicker training will work. And you will quickly be reassured of the incredible power in that little, plastic gadget known as a clicker!

Moving forward with your first training sessions

Once your intelligent pooch has been fully loaded, the sky's the limit with what you can do with clicker training! Both you and your dog will start looking forward to the training sessions.

A good first training "session" can be done in a very simple and informal manner. Be sure you have your clicker with you. Offer your pup his favorite snack. Normally, most dogs will come to you and perhaps sit and wait expecting you to give the treat. Make him wait a few seconds while you closely observe his movements.

Within seconds, he will get anxious and fidgety. You are looking closely to see what the first thing he does – Bark? Turn his head? The first thing you see him do, "click and treat". At this first training session, the behavior you choose to reward is not important. But, be careful not reward bad behavior, such as jumping up on your leg.

Whatever you rewarded, wait for him to do it again, and immediately click and treat. Wait. He will do it again. Click and treat. You will have fun doing this, and you can even start at this early stage, to try to shape his behavior.

After a few clicks and treats, when he does it again, wait a few seconds before clicking. He will likely do it again, thinking maybe you missed it! As soon as he does it a second time, click and treat. You have just shaped his behavior from one movement to two movements before he received his click and treat.

At this point, just for fun, try to introduce a command. Once he has demonstrated his understanding that he will get clicked and treated for his specific behavior, watch him closely. Just as soon as you see him starting to repeat the behavior, give a command. If you've been rewarding him for speaking, then right before he barks, say "Speak!" Then, immediately click and treat.

Another first training session idea is developing your dog's attention. Since dog's think about whatever it is they are looking at, you can train your dog to look at you and give you their full attention using these clicker training methods.

Have your dog, your clicker and treats, and a quiet place ready to go. Hold the clicker in one hand. In the other hand, have a treat. Hold that treat up to your face. Wait for your dog to look at you, then immediately click and treat. Repeat this process several times.

If she becomes distracted or loses focus, first hold the treat in front of her nose and slowly raise the treat to your face. When she is looking at you, click and treat. If you repeat this sequence twenty to twenty-five sessions, you will have effectively trained her to give you her attention.

Using these introductory steps, you can see the power of clicker training and proceed to more advanced training sessions. Watching you pooch's behavior change right before your eyes is amazing and fun. Enjoy your first training session! Your dog certainly will.

Chapter 4: Targeting

A logical next step in mastering the art of clicker training is to teach your dog the fine art of "targeting". This process is great for new clicker trainers because it is a relatively easy behavior to teach. Equally important, targeting is fun for both the dog and for you.

What is "targeting"? It is the process wherein you teach your dog to touch a target for a click and treat. The good thing about targeting is that you can use virtually any object for a target. You can be elaborate and purchase target sticks, which are commonly used by professional dog trainers. The dog is trained to touch, then follow the sticks. These can be very effective for training Seeing Eye dogs, for instance.

However, for the non-professional trainer, any object will do. When you want to teach your dog to "high five" you, you can use the palm of your hand as a target. You can also use objects like a pencil or even a piece of paper or your own fingertip as targets. Use your imagination.

Basic steps to do to teach the art of targeting

First, run through your preparation list. As always, have your clicker and treats ready. Before starting, decide on the target you are going to use. For this discussion, the palm of the hand will be the target. Only teach one target at a time. Before introducing another target, be sure your pup has mastered the first one.

Second, stand or kneel in front of your dog. Use a highly scented favorite treat, and rub some of it onto your palm. You want to be sure the scent of the treat is rubbed onto your palm so your dog can easily detect it.

With the treats in your other hand, encourage him to sniff your palm. Do this by quickly bringing your hand up, palm facing him, and bring it close to his nose. Click and treat for any movement he makes toward your hand – for looking at it; for sniffing or licking it; even for just touching it. Immediately click and treat.

Be sure you click at the exact time he does the behavior. If you are late, don't click. Praise him and continue.

Repeat this several times, but each time move your hand away from him a little distance. As he moves toward it or touches it, click and treat. Now, practice by holding your hand in different positions. Try holding it near the floor, above his head, to his right and to his left. Click and treat each time he touches your palm.

Keep moving it away from him so he has to take steps to come toward it to touch it. Click and treat as he steps in that direction. Some trainers believe that dogs will learn faster if they get clicked and receive the treat while they are moving. Practice different variations of this with your hand.

Try to get the pup to do more complex movements to get to your smelly palm. Maybe try to get him to stand on his back two legs to reach your hand. Or try holding your palm low to make him bow down to touch it. Keep the movements small at first. It is important to make reaching and touching the target easy, and not a hard task for the dog to master.

If you find that your dog is losing interest during the targeting session, it may be because the scent has worn off your hand. Be sure to rub more treat on it regularly during the training session to keep his interest. On the other hand, if your dog is catching on quickly, perhaps wagging his tail and eagerly trying to get to your hand, you can raise the bar. Since he has demonstrated he is capable of reliably touching your hand, have some fun varying the training.

Consider making him touch your palm two, or even three, times before the click and treat. Use your other hand to vary the training. Try adding a command. As soon as you put your hand out, say, "Touch". When he does so, click and treat. Repeat with this command several times with an immediate click and treat each time he successful touches your palm.

It is also important not to click and treat if your dog is doing something you do not want them to do. For example, if they come to your hand and mouth your hand or bite it, omit the click and treat. If they touch your wrist or somewhere other than your palm, omit the click and treat. Your smart pooch will quickly learn what behavior you are trying to get him to do and which one you do not like. An "omitted click" is a great signal to him that that behavior is not the right one!

Advanced target training is used effectively to train dogs to do more involved behaviors. By using the command "touch", you can teach your dog to touch other things, as well. Using yellow sticky notes, and training your dog to touch them, allows you to stick them wherever you want the dog to touch. The dogs can be trained to turn on and off light switches, or to retrieve remote controls. They can easily be taught to retrieve objects by name using targeting. Military dogs, police dogs, and agility trainers use advanced target training extensively.

For target training, keeping the sessions short is especially important. Three to four minutes a few times a day will work well and be very effective. At the same time, this will keep the dog interested and looking forward to the next session. Teaching your dog to touch a target with his nose on cue is fun to do. Enjoy watching him learn!

Chapter 5: Teaching Your Dog Specific Behaviors

Moving forward with more training is somewhat intimidating, but exciting at the same time. Once you see how quickly your dog learns using clicker training, you almost cannot wait to proceed to another new behavior to teach them! Here are some guidelines for training your pup to do some common specific behaviors using the clicker. (You can use whichever hand you desire, but for these instructions, we will assume a right-handed person is doing the training.)

NOTE: All dogs will make mistakes or move not perform the behavior you are teaching. For those instances, simply say, in a neutral, non-threatening, non-shouting voice, "Wrong" or even "Uh-uh" (both are better than no – no can be threatening or even get confused with other words more easily than these two words). Then, try again.

Another important point to keep in mind: When using verbal cues, only say the word one time. Do not keep repeating it. For example, say, "Sit", not "Sit..sit..sit.." Or, while a dog is in the stay position, do not keep saying, "Stay..stay..stay.." Repeating the command in this manner only serves to confuse the dog.

Using clicker training, most trainers are amazed at the speed with which dogs learn these behaviors.

1. Teaching your dog to sit:

The clicker is held in the left hand. The treat is held in the right hand. You want to maneuver your dog into the sitting position. Hold the treat in front of her nose and slowly raise the treat in an arc. This will "lure" him into a sitting position.

At this stage, there is no need to use the verbal command, "Sit". Timing is the most critical issue at this point.

The instant your dog sits, click and treat. Many trainers suggest you watch your dog closely, and the precise instant they "start to move into the sitting position", you click and treat. This is an excellent habit for you to develop, as it insures you will not be late with the click.

Repeat this sit exercise at least fifteen to twenty times. This will only take a few minutes, but that will be the complete session. Ordinarily, you will do this same session one more time. Depending on the dog's learning capability, once you feel they have mastered the sit using no verbal commands, proceed to the next session.

At the next session, do the exact same steps. However, at the precise instant your dog starts to move into the sit position, say "Sit", followed immediately with click and treat.

2. Teaching your dog to stay:

The clicker and treat are held as in the sit training session. Get your pup into the sitting position. Stand in front of her and say, "Stay". When she holds her position for even a few seconds, click and treat.

If she gets up or makes any movements to start to get up, say "Wrong". Repeat the stay command, and when she stays, click and treat. Repeat this at least five times per session. Each repetition, try to increase the length of stay by a few seconds before the click and treat.

Also, try moving yourself with very small steps in front of her. If she holds her stay position while you are moving, instantly click and treat. It is a good exercise for teaching the dog to be disciplined if you introduce movement. Be sure to immediately click and reward.

If she hears the click and makes a move to come out of her stay, do not give the treat. Rather, lure her back into a sit position, and then give the treat.

Begin increasing the time she stays before you click and treat. Repeat and increase the time at least five times per session. Your goal is to get her to hold her stay position for at least one minute. It is important to vary the lengths of time you ask her to stay. Click and treat after a couple long stays, then click and treat after a few short stays. Depending on what your training goals are, you can gradually increase the time intervals you ask her to stay.

Once you are confident she can stay for one minute, you can start adding distance between you and her. It is best to train only one behavior at a time, so, when adding distance, do not ask her to do long stays at the same time. Add distance, and click and treat after a short stay.

When she can stay for the length of time you want, and she can stay when you are at the distance you want, then, and only then, is it appropriate to combine the two behaviors. Staying is not a natural behavior for dogs, so be patient and gradually increase your demands. You will be amazed at the results.

3. Teaching your dog to leave something:

Another great thing about clicker training is that it can be effective in eliminating unwanted behavior. This is an important behavior to teach, as most dogs are curious creatures.

Teaching the "leave it" behavior can help in those instances when: your dog is heading toward an ugly pile of debris on the sidewalk and is considering eating it; or when you drop something on the floor that you do not want them to have; or for those dogs who are prone to coprophagia (eating their own feces).

Get some tasty treats and put them in your right hand, which will be your "leave it" hand. Put an even tastier treat in your left hand, which will be your click and treat hand.

Get down to the dog's level and hold your right hand open with the treats in your hand. The instant he moves to get the treats, close your fist around them. Do not pull your hand away. Keep it at his level. He will no doubt investigate your fist smelling and maybe licking to get to them.

When he backs off and moves away from your fist, immediately click and treat from your left hand. Repeat this until he associates moving away from your hand with the treat reward.

Now, show the hand with the treat on the open palm and say, "Leave it" as you move to the dog's level. If he leaves it or turns away, click and treat. If he goes for the treat, quickly close the hand and wait for him to move away as he did before. Repeat, until he figures out to leave the treat in the open hand.

Practice this by setting targets and clicking and rewarding him when he responds to your "leave it" command. The next time you are out and about, and he approaches a dead worm on the sidewalk, give the "leave it" command. At this point, he should have it ingrained in his brain to actually leave it. Even if you do not have the clicker and treats, immediately reward him with hugs, praise, and any treats you may have!

4. Teaching your dog to walk or run from point A to point B:

This training involves teaching your dog to leave you and go to another location. Some trainers call it a "send out" or a "go out". Its purpose is to train her to get from one point to another on command.

For this session, most trainers use an inexpensive target arrow (like those used for target practice in archery), a rubber ball or plastic whiffle golf ball with holes in it, a clicker, and treats.

Press the arrow through the ball and slide it up the arrow's shaft. Introduce your dog to the arrow. Hold the arrow and ball and move the ball end down to the dog's nose and say, "Touch". This will be similar to your targeting exercises you have already mastered! When his nose touches the ball, click and treat. Repeat this several times.

Now, stick the arrowhead into the ground and move the ball up the shaft to the level of your dog's nose. Then, stand close to the arrow, and repeat the touch exercise. Click and treat when he bumps the ball. Repeat until he associates touching the ball with a treat.

Next, increase the distance each time by stepping back a step each time. So, the sequence will be: you say, "touch"; your dog moves to the ball and bumps it with his nose; you then click at the exact moment his nose touches the ball; the dog comes back to you; you reward him with a treat.

Your goal should be to move to a distance of ten yards and consistently be able to complete the exercise. You will then have successfully trained your pooch to walk or run from point A (your side) to point B (the ball on the arrow shaft).

Using these techniques of clicker training, you can easily vary your training to adapt it to many different scenarios. Down, down/stay, shaking hands, rolling over, etc., are all easily taught to the clicker-ready dog.

You can also use these techniques to teach more advanced behaviors, such as retrieving named objects. This is done by teaching the complex behaviors in a specific sequence and in a gradual manner. This is known as "shaping" the behavior. This is nothing more than breaking down the complex, final behavior you are teaching into smaller, easier to learn steps.

Chapter 6: How to Use Signals

As we have seen, most professional clicker trainers simply use the clicker as the only signal when initially teaching new behaviors. Traditional training methods train by first giving the command, and then teaching the pooch what the command means. With clicker training, any commands, verbal or non-verbal, are only introduced after the dog is reliably performing the new behavior.

Effective use of non-verbal signals

In actuality, the click of the clicker is a non-verbal signal. So, as you begin your clicker training adventure, you can readily see that dogs respond very well to non-verbal signals. Once you have clicker trained your dog to perform a behavior, you can easily introduce other signals.

The luring motions used to move your dog into certain positions (moving your hand in an arc motion to move him into a sitting position for example) are easily adapted into hand signals. If you are using food as your lure, once the dog is reliably performing a behavior, you can eliminate the food lure and train with the hand motion alone.

When your dog associates the hand signal to the desired behavior, he will be able to respond to the hand signal appropriately. The trainer will click the behavior only when it is performed in response to the hand signal. Dog trainers often believe that hand signals are easier for dogs to learn than are verbal signals.

The technique for teaching the use of non-verbal signals is as follows:

First determine what behavior you want to teach your dog at that particular session. Then run through a few repetitions of that behavior with your clicks and treats.

When you feel your dog is ready, give him a non-verbal signal when he performs the desired behavior, and click and treat. Some trainers recommend you put the new hand signal in front of a verbal command.

Repeat this fifteen to twenty times with your dog. Then, continue using only the hand signal without the verbal command. Repeat several repetitions using only hand signals.

An important aspect to the use of hand signals involves motion. Your hand signals will work best if they include movement that actually changes the silhouette your dog sees. The motion of your hand is easier to follow, and therefore, easier for your dog to learn and remember. Also, each time you practice a session, vary the use of verbal and non-verbal signals.

Teaching your dog hand signals makes your clicker training much easier. Your pup will be much better able to comprehend what it is you want him to perform during your clicker training sessions when he understands your hand signals.

Effective use of verbal signals

Many newcomers to clicker training are mystified by the fact that this training technique is performed without speaking to the dog! They do not initially realize that the sound of the click is the only signal needed to successfully train the dog.

However, clicker trainers readily include the use of verbal signals in their training modalities. But, these verbal cues are not introduced until the dogs are capable of performing the desired behaviors in response to the clicker.

The teaching of verbal signals is essentially the same as the teaching of non-verbal signals. First, decide the behavior you want to teach at that session. Run through several repetitions of the clicker training you have used for that behavior in past sessions.

Once your dog understands the behavior you desire at that particular session, introduce verbal signals. For example, if you are teaching the sit behavior, the precise instant he moves into the sit position, say, "Sit", and immediately click and treat.

Repeat that sequence ten to fifteen times. You will begin to see that your dog will take less and less time to sit between the time you give the command and the time he actually sits! That is when you know he understands the command.

Another use of verbal signals involves using words to stop or correct a behavior. These words are as important as the verbal commands you teach your dog. Using the same training scenario, if your dog does not respond to your click or verbal command to sit, you should use a verbal cue such as "Wrong". Keep these verbal corrections in a neutral, non-threatening voice. Another effective verbal correction is the command to "leave it" discussed earlier.

Dogs are very adept at learning commands, whether they are verbal or non-verbal. But, these commands are learned even more readily when coupled with clicker training.

Chapter 7: Common Myths About Clicker Training

No method of training an animal is perfect. Period. There are pro's and con's about all animal training protocols. Clicker training is no different.

Clicker training is a fun, exciting, accelerated learning program that has well-documented success. Is it the only training recommended by experts? Of course not. But, there are so many positive attributes to clicker training that is important to look at some of the misunderstood aspects of this positive reinforcement animal training method.

1. Clickers are not needed to train dogs since voice commands work the same.

The clicker and its distinct clicking sound is not some magical sound. It is merely a unique, clear and consistent sound. On the other hand, the human voice speaking voice commands can be highly variable.

If the trainer is excited, the excitement will always come through when speaking. If angry, that emotion can be detected in the human voice. The same is true for a variety of other human emotions. You are only human. There is no way you can emit a consistent, unique command every time you speak it. The clicker can and does.

Additionally, using the clicker insures you deliver a precisely timed sound to mark good behavior. That precise timing makes the use of the clicker more effective than the human voice commands.

Obviously, using voice commands to train dogs can and do work. They have been used for centuries with success. However, studies have shown that clicker trained dogs were superior to dogs trained with verbal commands in behavior acquisition, and they also required fewer reinforcements.

2. Clicker training requires that I have to carry treats and the clicker with me at all times.

This is a very common concern that people have about clicker training. They are worried they will have to have a pouch of smelly treats attached to their belts wherever they go.

This could not be further from the truth. It is imperative to remember that clicker training is a "construction" method. It is primarily used in the beginning stages of training known as the acquisition phase. Once the animal has "acquired" the requisite behavior, the clicker can be phased out.

Eventually, the clicker can be replaced with positive verbal markers. Since the dog has already learned the behavior through the use of the clicker, this is usually an easy transition. And, you can unstrap your treat pouch at that time!

3. Clicker training is only good for teaching a dog tricks.

It is very true that you can teach your dog some really neat tricks using clicker training. And, you can do it in a rapid fashion.

But, clicker training is a highly effective dog training method used by thousands of professionals around the world. Police dogs and military dogs are often trained with this method. If clicker training was only for teaching tricks, this would not be the case. In fact, this type of training can teach a multitude of new behaviors that are not trick behaviors.

Equally important, clicker training can also be used to correct specific behavioral problems. By using a clicker to mark desired behavior, negative behavior can be corrected. Clicking and treating the desired behavior is a distinct signal to the dog that that is the behavior you want.

4. When taking clicker training classes with other dogs, my dog will be distracted by all the other clicking sounds.

This is a legitimate concern. After all, if you are paying to have your dog trained or to learn how to train him using clicker training, you do not want him to be distracted.

While this is an understandable concern, it has been shown over and over that your dog will not be distracted by all the other clicks. Dogs have superb hearing. They are very proficient at discerning which click belongs to their owner.

Since you would have already loaded the clicker, your pooch is conditioned to his clicker. Amazingly, they are quite proficient at sorting out the clicks and do not get confused about which click will result in the positive reinforcer in the form of a tasty treat.

5. Clicker training requires that my dog be fed multiple treats throughout the day that will cause her to unnecessarily gain weight.

Firs, clicker training does suggest using small food treats as the positive reinforcer. Although, you can use other forms of positive reinforcement, such as praise or touch.

But, for newcomers to clicker training, bite-sized food treats are not only convenient for the trainer, but also good motivators for most dogs. It is strongly emphasized by all clicker training programs that the treats used be small, and hence low in calories. Many trainers recommend substituting a mealtime for a training session to avoid the problem of possibly over-feeding your dog. And, finally, remember that the sessions are very short, not requiring the use of an inordinate amount of the treats, and the dog is exercising at the same time he is getting the "extra" calories.

For these reasons, weight gain is not usually a result of a properly conducted clicker-training program.

Chapter 8: Frequently Asked Questions

1. I have an older dog. Is it too late to train him using clicker training?

This is a very common question, perhaps due to the age-old saying, "You can't teach an old dog new tricks." A wonderful thing about licker training is that it can be used for dogs of almost any age. Puppies respond very will to clicker training. They may require a little more patience on your part, but they are eager learners.

Remember, when working with very young puppies keep your sessions shorter. They have not developed the attention span of a more mature dog. Try shorter, more frequent training sessions.

Even older, more mature dogs can be trained with the clicker. The issue is not the dog's age. What is important is that you are a patient, persistent, and consistent clicker trainer. Dogs of all ages will benefit from clicker training. Try it on all ages!

2. Do I have to use "store-bought" treats?

Commercial dog treats are not required for clicker training. In fact, many professional trainers encourage homemade treats over "store-bought" treats. The primary reason for this is the tastiness factor. It is critical that the treats you use for clicker training be very tasty. Tasty enough to insure they will keep your dog interested during the entire session. You want your dog to be motivated by the anticipation of a wonderful treat.

The more they like and look forward to your treats, the easier will be your training sessions. For this reason, many trainers use, and encourage you to use, homemade treats. There are numerous suggestions for what type of treat to use. Online resources can be very helpful.

In general, think healthy and think about what your dog likes. You can use small bits of cheese, hot dogs, beef, etc. Making your own treats allows you to be creative and to insure variety. Your pooch will be more apt to look forward to the training session if he expects a tasty treat. Keep him guessing about what you made for the next session!

3. I don't have a lot of time to spend training my dog. Will it take me a long time to learn and to train him using clicker training methods?

Another benefit of clicker training is that it is very easy to learn and to do. Even a total novice can learn how to train their dog with a clicker. If you follow the instructions on how to do proper clicker training, either via your self-instruction or with a trainer, it will not take long to learn.

Once you have learned the initial stages you must use, which involve clicker handling, treat delivery, and timing, the actual training with your pooch will easily flow. You will be amazed at how fast you learn how to train, and even more importantly, how fast your dog learns!

4. My dog is notoriously resistant to being trained. How do I know if clicker training will work for my dog?

Rest assured that proper clicker training methods can be used successfully with any dog. Even hard-to-train dogs have been shown to respond very well to the clicker. Any type of dog, from your mixed breed, sweet-faced "mutt" to your high stepping show dog, clicker training can work effectively. Even the hardened police and rescue dogs are often trained with clicker training.

Rescue dogs are frequently very easy to train using the clicker training methods. They often have been mistreated and have developed behavioral problems before being rescued. The beauty of using clicker training for these dogs is that this type of training is a very effective way to teach new, more appropriate behaviors to these rescue dots.

5. I have been conscientious about training my dog since she was a puppy. I am very intrigued by clicker training. Would clicker training work with her since she has already been trained?

Professional clicker trainers love to introduce the clicker to dogs who have been trained via more traditional methods. Often these trainers recommend starting your clicker training by teaching her a brand new behavior. Since your dog has been used to training sessions and has already learned other behaviors, teaching her a new behavior will convince you of the usefulness of clicker training.

Traditionally trained dogs who may have been previously timid about their training sessions often become eager learners using clicker training. Clicker training could be a very effective training method for your well-trained dog.

6. Since clicker training requires the use of food treats, will I have to use food every time I want him to respond?

Absolutely not. If you closely follow the recommended training methods for clicker training your dog, you will learn how to vary your reinforcements. Starting with food treats is recommended. However, you can effectively introduce other positive reinforcers once you are confident that your pooch has learned the behavior you are introducing.

Since you will not have treats with you at all times, your clicker-trained dog will have learned how to respond to your other positive reinforcers. Having built the foundation using the clicker and food treats, you pup will become very adept at responding to your commands.

7. How many sessions will it take for my dog to begin to learn new behaviors?

The answer to this can be somewhat variable. Of course, like humans, every dog is different, so there is no absolute answer to this question. However, clicker training has been studied extensively using numerous different types and ages of dogs. So, normal time periods for achieving success using clicker-training period have been well documented.

If you follow the instructions carefully when doing your clicker training, you will find that your dog will learn simple behaviors or tricks in as few as one or two training sessions. For example, teaching sit or shaking hands are often learned very quickly.

Clicker training can be used to coax a dog along a specific path to "shape" a behavior one step at a time. Even though each training session is less than ten or fifteen minutes, you may need a number of sessions to shape a new behavior, such as those behaviors taught to Seeing-Eye dogs. Teaching a Seeing-Eye dog to turn off a light switch is a much more complex behavior to teach than just training them to come.

As your dog becomes more accustomed to clicker training, they will be eager to learn new and more advanced behaviors. Experiment and enjoy!

8. My son is only eleven years old. Is he too young to use clicker training on our two-year-old dog?

Your son should absolutely get involved in clicker training your pooch! One of the great benefits of clicker training is that, unlike traditional training methods, it does not make any one person in the family the "pack leader". So, dogs learn to respond equally well to all family members.

This is why everyone in your family should get involved in using the clicker training methods to train your dog. There are different recommendations on how a family should do the training. Generally, only one or two members should train at any one given session. Everyone needs to be consistent with the training and follow the clicker training techniques exactly.

There are really no drawbacks to letting your children get involved in the fun. Clicker training is a positive reinforcement technique. It can be very beneficial to your children to see dogs trained in a humane, fun, and positive manner. Start a generation of positive trainers!

9. I have a three-pound Papillion who is very skittish about loud noises. How can I use clicker training to train her?

Many dogs are somewhat jumpy when they hear loud, sharp noises. It is in their nature to be alert to possible dangers that may accompany new, loud sounds. So, your pooch is not different from many others.

There are some easy solutions to this dilemma. First, try holding the clicker in your hand and keeping that hand in your pocket. When you click, the sound will be muffled and not quite as loud and sharp sounding to your dog.

Secondly, if the muted click from your pocket does not work, try several different types of clickers. They all have unique sounds of varying loudness. If you can find one that does not cause your dog to be jumpy or scared, your problem is solved.

Finally, it is noteworthy that even deaf dogs can be trained using a modified version of clicker training. Many professional dog trainers who employ clicker-training methods will substitute a quick flash of light for the sound of the clicker. All other aspects of clicker training can be used in the same manner. For your skittish dog, if the previous suggestions do not work, you could try this method, which is essentially silent. Hence, no loud clicks to make your pup uneasy!

10. What is the best way to get started to learn how to clicker train my dog?

You have a number of great options from which to choose to get started in your clicker training adventure. The option you choose depends on your personal situation.

If you want to do it all yourself, a great place to start is via online searches. There are a great number of sites online which can provide a wide variety of training options. Reading articles and viewing YouTube videos will give you a wealth of easy to follow information to get you started. If you are a disciplined self-learner, these can be very effective tools.

However, if you do not want to do it yourself, and want to learn from a professional, there are several places to look. Larger metropolitan areas will likely have several trainers from which to choose. Even if you live in a rural location, you can consult online resources, your phone book, your veterinarian, and even local pet stores for names of professional dog trainers in your area.

Many professional trainers may encourage you to train with them using traditional methods. Be sure to stipulate that you want to learn how to train your dog using "clicker training".

Conclusion

As you can see from the information in this guide, clicker training is a well-established and respected method of dog training. The sound scientific basis upon which it is based gives this type of training legitimacy. Dog trainers worldwide are hailing the virtues of clicker training for animals.

Using the non-emotional and consistent sounding click emitted from the clicker is a super way to make your dog stay alert and interested in the training session. The click and treat methodology you use is so motivating that your pooch will actually look forward to the next training session. No more drudgery, just fun and exciting training sessions for both you and your dog.

There are multiple ways to train your dog. Perhaps the biggest seller for clicker training is that is a positive reinforcement training method that does not rely on force (such as leash pulling or choke collars), punishment, or any negative methods to achieve great results. Because of this, clicker training can safely be used to train young puppies, skittish or jumpy dogs, and any dog of any breed.

As is true with any training method, the trainer (you!) must have patience and persistence in their repertoire. You will most certainly experience the "joy of victory and the agony of defeat". But, when at first you don't succeed, clicker training allows you to easily try, try, and try again.

Of all training methods, clicker training will give you the most rapid results. This makes clicker training a very appealing training method for beginning trainers. The short, ten to fifteen minute training sessions are very easy for the novice to manage. Neither the trainer nor the pooch get "burned out" or exhausted during these short sessions as can commonly occur with traditional training methods.

With so many advantages and so few disadvantages, one wonders why clicker training is not more prevalent. The advantages are for the dogs and for the trainers. For the dogs, clicker training allows them to be more intimately engaged in the actual training sessions.

The mental stimulation that clicker training provides is a major advantage for your dog. And, since there is no punishment involved for doing wrong, the dogs actually look forward to performing behaviors that will bring them a positive reward.

For the trainer, he can enjoy training without having to use force or punishment. The fact that clicker training is quickly learned makes it appealing to all dog owners. And, most dog owners are elated to be able to train their beloved dogs using positive reinforcement and upbeat methods. The trainers will truly appreciate the improved communication that results using clicker training. Additionally, this positive type of training ultimately leads to deeper bond between the dog and the trainer.

Clicker training is a truly enjoyable and exciting way to effectively train your dog. You will most certainly get better at it the more you use it. Each time you see your efforts result in your dog learning new tricks or behaviors will give you great satisfaction.

For anyone who wants to better understand his or her dog and enjoy watching their furry friends play, think and learn, clicker training is ideal! Whether you are teaching the simple concepts of sitting or staying, or a more complex task such as turning off light switches, you can most certainly have fun training your dog using this training method. The simplicity of clicker training, the ease with which it is learned, and the ease with which it is employed make it the training method of choice for all manner of trainers, from the seasoned professional to the know-nothing novice!

Jump in and enjoy the fun of clicker training your dog!

Made in the USA
San Bernardino, CA
12 September 2016